How To Find All Missing Persons / Unsolved Cases. And Collect All Reward Offers. Volume X1. THE CASE OF ANNE CECILLE ZAPPELLI

DAVID GOMADZA

www.twofuture.world

Copyright © 2024 David Gomadza

All rights reserved.

PAPERBACK ISBN: 9798326494306

DEDICATION

CONTENTS

Acknowledgments

How To Find All Missing Persons / Unsolved Cases.
And Collect All Reward Offers. Volume XI.
THE CASE OF ANNE CECILLE ZAPPELLI   1

The Afterlife Conversation and The Council Of Creation.   3

The Killers.   20

ACKNOWLEDGMENTS

Tomorrow's World Order

How To Find All Missing Persons / Unsolved Cases. And Collect All Reward Offers. Volume XI. THE CASE OF ANNE CECILLE ZAPPELLI

BACKGROUND INFORMATION

CASE

CATEGORY

$1m Reward, Cold Cases

DATE

22 Sep 1969

DESCRIPTION:

20 years of age.

Fair complexion.

How To Find All Missing Persons / Unsolved Cases. And Collect All Reward Offers.
Volume XI. THE CASE OF ANNE CECILLE ZAPPELLI

Thin build

Blonde hair

Wearing a white woolen frock, stockings and black shoes.

QUICK CASE FACTS:

Miss Zappelli lived in Morawa with her family.
Was in Geraldton for Post Office examinations.

Went to the Oasis drive-in with three others.

Left by herself at 11:00pm.

Reported missing at 8:30am on 23 September 1969.

Body located on 24 September 1969.

BACKGROUND:

Anne Cecille Zappelli, was born in May 1949, lived with her parents in Morawa, a town situated about 160km's inland from Geraldton, where she worked at the local post office exchange.

Miss Zappelli was a popular person in Morawa and held in high regard by all who knew her.

CASE DETAILS:

On Wednesday 17 September 1969, Miss Zappelli went to Geraldton with a number of other people to sit for postal examinations, scheduled to finish on 23 September 1969.

How To Find All Missing Persons / Unsolved Cases. And Collect All Reward Offers.
Volume XI. THE CASE OF ANNE CECILLE ZAPPELLI

On the evening of Monday 22 September, Miss Zappelli went to the Oasis Drive-in (pictured), situated in Rowe Street, Wonthella (Geraldton) to watch the movie 'Counterpoint' along with her female roommate and two male friends.

Around 11:00pm, prior to the conclusion of the movie, Miss ZAPPELLI left her acquaintances, walking alone down Rowe Street (now North West Coastal Highway). She did not have a purse or handbag in her possession.

This was the last time Miss Zappelli was seen alive.

Miss ZAPPELLI was reported as a missing person around 8:30am Tuesday 23 September.

LOCATED:

At about 1:25pm on Wednesday 24 September 1969, the body of Miss Zappelli was discovered 50 metres off Rowe Street and 300 metres south of Bayly Street, Geraldton.

A post mortem examination revealed that it was likely Miss Zappelli was murdered soon after leaving the drive inn.

The person or persons responsible for Miss ZAPPELLI's murder have not yet been identified. If you have any information about the murder of Anne Cecille Zappelli, please contact Crime Stoppers on 1800 333 000 or make an online report below.

TOMORROW'S WORLD ORDER'S PERSPECTIVES

THE AFTERLIFE CONVERSATION AND THE COUNCIL OF CREATION'S ANAYLSIS

I was killed I was my vagina removed while alive my God help the trauma alone kills it was a night out last day of the Retuvwxyz test [post office] that caused all this they told me they wanted someone else who wanted a better pay and less hours I said yes at first they said you are only 20 and I said okay so what they said you must be 22 I said two years training at half the salary then backdated it 1 year they said you are clever and asked me to tell everyone that for you they were willing to bend some rules so I agreed and said I can come with you when I finished because he was a man and he looked lost and I said to the party I heard there is a party after this and he said I will but if you can then it's wise to keep this professional because if someone think I gave you because there is sex involved that will be bad because I am married and I will be sacked and I giggled when he said married and he said what's funny and I said they are telling people that we can be partners as a joke no one had said that and he said why ruin a great opportunity I want to prove that we can be equal with women without sex involved so please respect that and let me know what can be of the future I am glad because I will get a huge bonus and a promotion to another town and he said this will be bad if I have to lose all that for a vagina and I spread my legs and looked at it and said no one loses a vagina

How To Find All Missing Persons / Unsolved Cases. And Collect All Reward Offers. Volume XI. THE CASE OF ANNE CECILLE ZAPPELLI

unless but and he looked lost and said you challenging me [now I call you bitch secretly] and he said I can whatever you bring but so let's dropped this and say byes because I want to work with you I told my wife about you and I got grumpy and just walked out but he said wait no one can lose a dick either so that cancels your bet we are square and I said okay if you like then we can just go as friends my two friends are coming it will be great pickup 8pm tonight come back 12 am okay bye and he got up and walked out and now he said what can be can be and he left but holding his dick that day I went home and shaved just my vagina and looked at it really for a first time and said if we can we can but then I looked at it in the mirror and it literally said enjoy me before someone take it with a hacksaw and I felt scare but that aroused me that for the first time I asked it what it wanted and said what do you like it said I am just a vagina once someone cum inside that's it your bet might cost me my life so I laughed and said who believe a talking vagina and it said yeah talking because when it's last hours everything on you talks and I said last hours for being me and it said I want you to make me so horny this person would rather fuck than cut who bets about her own body parts stupid girl you are and now if you come out alive with your vagina then he has to lose his dick a person helping you why would you do that Anne I ask and I need an answer if I were human this is the time I slap you hard if I have a dick and bend you down and say you wish my vagina gone then have dick in first and enjoy last journey to hell because whoever is going to cut it will have to be ruthless so that you go to heaven on pity but then if it's not violent enough you must go to heaven 9but now while the vagina talk deep inside me I started to realise that I was really luck for some reason for the first time I could here my body parts talk and the nipple said stop sending nrtuvxyzprstuvwxyz unless you are prepared to touch me as well otherwise fuck my arse arsehole and I literally laughed I said who taught you that vulgar language and it said aty and pointed at me in the mirror so I said aty where are you and instantly I vibrated like a blood phone mind you this is the 1960s then I said what can be of us and it said too late everything think you are now fucking late because the challenges have been

How To Find All Missing Persons / Unsolved Cases. And Collect All Reward Offers.
Volume XI. THE CASE OF ANNE CECILLE ZAPPELLI

sent to a new source and the source said can I fuck it first therefore make it really horny and it said spread and let me see but it sound like the opposite sex and somehow it said I can if you can but and I said maybe tonight but and it said what about humping now bend down and it's in lie and the vagina drops dead and I laughed but it made an annoyed lip sound and said if we can't then who can and I said I can but and it said no buts bend down now save vagina I try and I said no before it finished then it said I can but and I said but no but and it got angry and kicked about literally vibrating my legs and I said I now want to save pussy but once and forever peace and it said only once then no let vagina die instead then you will understand then I said what could be and then it said about what and I said about life and it said for me just beginning as yours just ending because after tonight there will never be another life for you you can't think about important things for example can you give arse to safe vagina if vagina is not well and sex can kill it can't you give arse? If no then how can you pass tonight no chance so let's teach you what we do when you apply positions you ate not entitled to then set up a good honest man who worked hard to help you now you want to smear that person with sex and when he introduced you to his wife this is wrong I can't accept this today you must apologize and mean it to both now I will bring his wife which was not supposed to happen but just happened and say this is wrong repent or die there is no other option but I can feel your xyztrstuvwxyzrstuvwstrt as denying all this as childish [brain but small and immature] Now I am a honest man as well when I heard what you said I died inside you work hard but then lose your head after you got the job why and I said I got the job as in asking and he said yes but death can come too because I don't know why you did it but once I know why you did it then I will decide whether you live or die and at this point I got upset and said bitch be like me no what if and he instantly opened his eyes in disgust and said I can do it myself if you want without all this playing games artestern is my brother and can do you for him okay don't ever think you can do shit on me because shit can do you literally like but if we can't then you win I leave this county of Restoprstuvwxyz [stenopqrst

How To Find All Missing Persons / Unsolved Cases. And Collect All Reward Offers.
Volume XI. THE CASE OF ANNE CECILLE ZAPPELLI

Australia code 84389828678928019806838901234589l0] Now if I Ask what can be of this I said we can but and he said if we can't then I will leave once he said that I relaxed because it started to sound like he wanted sex but himself with me and it started to make sense he is the one who wants vagina his brother wants just arse now if I look at this back now it sounded a love triangle but there was no love here at all because 8pm he came instead and said I want to know what you are thinking asking my young brother for a job you don't deserve then go on to make it look like he didn't deserve I felt so low I bent down and took off my knickers and said I agree to just once and so come and let's go I did not plan all this I was so nervous with him and he got up of the couch and lifted me by the chin and said I am a jew do you know jews and I murmured and said due what and he said okay lay on your stomach I want missionary and he went out so thought just once we do and go I had no idea that he meant jew people I knew jews but what did jews have to do with this are they not people so he said can we now on return but he brought his brother with him the one I longed since I started working there and he smiled and said this was the test see you can do this to any man even my brother then what do you want I gave you the job already now you still persist with me now my brother etc so I say my final decision is no I might have considered two wives but it's too late I warned you about the test then what and I said he said arse only so no big deal vagina only you and I looked as if I don't care about him now and he said who are you you come in our lives now I was to propose that if you are serious we can be family but the three of us my religion does not restrict this so last test me or my brother then we go and I literally threw up and ran away without a word I said if it's arse I don't care if he want I can give him when he comes and he refused saying maybe I want as well that shocked all and he said okay let's go and talk there as time was nearly 8pm so I let them go first and changed and followed them on a bicycle now this is the funny part when I went to them now they were divided one brother to one side the vagina side the other in the arse side it sound so ridiculous that both fight for me before I even started the job now this is the sad part when I went to

How To Find All Missing Persons / Unsolved Cases. And Collect All Reward Offers.
Volume XI. THE CASE OF ANNE CECILLE ZAPPELLI

his brother for arse talk he sat on the table in front of us and said what if we can swap I get my brother back give him the job and get us back rather than pursue you with your everything that moves antiques so I said okay just you then but why so jealous he is your brother you think he don't fuck your wife he tell me he does he only say me arse he vagina and she said she cum hard with him than with you so I am like confused does that mean you don't know and he cried and said the reason why I want you and you want to repeat that with him oh my Yahweh I died twice but you want me or him why him every woman I get and why arse I am more religious than him so you should be loving me more than him but he said interrupting they all like the one who pumps hard and the arse don't mind hard rhythms but brother as a jew you know this is bad to Yahweh and the elder brother said I will ask Yahweh then he said Ya.ask.you.me.whats wrong with fucking arse [one word] .send.ya then instantly something came back as a hiccup sound and said through moving jaws as everyone heard it it matters most if you want children we want children free from defects you start intercrossing then cross contamination can happen if this does happen then a fertilized embroy will be defected resulting in crippling and other bad things so to a family man man and others it's subjective and depends on you
[Ya.ask.you.me.howdoiintroducemysel so ftotheworldasyahweh'srepresentative.send.ya
Say behold the day has come that you filthy people who corrupted by money and property will pay the consequences of abusing orphans and stealing their house so that you give to your officer for one life and four 4 I shall make sure that you will be reduced in size by that number meaning for every one of you there must be 4 of them not the current situation where they out number orphans not because orphaned is good no but because this is the right thing to do you must swear by me that before the year is over Yahweh will have had his vengeance and as such be prepared to fight all in all countries until death sets upon them for thus said the holy one of esreebel I will not stand and watch any more them ravaging toddlers and women for isreebrel was warned that if it does not

How To Find All Missing Persons / Unsolved Cases. And Collect All Reward Offers. Volume XI. THE CASE OF ANNE CECILLE ZAPPELLI

respect others children it risks being taken to hesboro and lanters and sqrstuvwxyztrsuvwxoy meaning Qatar now if they insist before 28 of June I will have got all rounded up and sent to the dungeons for thus said Yahweh the Almighty Ruler of the world exonerate davidgomadza as my representative and live ever happily after end of message
[Restart]
Now the night when I died something jumped in my throat and I woke up early as I wanted to be there first it was to start at 9pm so we were supposed to arrive at 8pm 6 pm I was up meaning I slept only from 3 pm after finishing work at 2pm I dressed up and suddenly a huge knock at the door woke me up and I said who are you knocking like a fuck police man and opened the door a man stood there and he said I can but and I am aremponsterst and I was given this address by antertops and I smiled because this is the man who had offered me a job early with 2 years and he said I am his rstuvwxystuvwerstuvw and I said okay I know brother and he smiled so he said what with you and my brother is this serious because he is married and they were fighting so this better be good and I said it is good and like all his wife I back them up and he shook his waist pretending to do me doggystyle and I said okay I can and he said what I said okay arse for you and vagina for him and he laughed and said you know i did this to his wife as a joke and now I sneak there to do her doggystyle and it sounded so real that I felt he wanted to do me before we even met and said okay come to the bedroom and let's try just once then we go but he laughed and said it's a joke but after he tried vagina maybe and I looked so embarrassed and said I will give you after we get married so he squints his left eye and said okay but a secret and quickly went back out and brought his brother and I could tell that he knew something had happened that he said if we can then and stopped I asked and said can what but and he looked confused and said what if I want but too then what when you offer it to my big brother he cursed and smiled instantly he said I can but then I said but no but we can only and he looked confused and said but mine no brother only me everything after baby then but and she said wait all that long why when he can but he threw a

How To Find All Missing Persons / Unsolved Cases. And Collect All Reward Offers.
Volume XI. THE CASE OF ANNE CECILLE ZAPPELLI

tantrum and said relationship for two and I looked at him and said when you with her he with me but but but but and brother but burn where are you and he looked furious than ever before and said then there could be something wrong with the vagina to give but to everyone and I laughed and said lose vagina but keep but only for brother then what's the point of the marriage and he got up and went and washed his face and legs and said Yahweh rstuvwxyzsters and cursed I said can we go now before they close us out before but and vagina even started moaning but vagina but vagina but vagina now I was about to say if they close maybe let's just stay here and but and vagina but as a joke and in no particular order so he said Yahweh urstuvwxyz I am mistaken for choice to love or to kill a wife that treats me like but but without love but one asking all the time now I am boiling for vagina and first thing to her is but and he said okay I lost again to my clever big brother because he keep checking all my women's butts so get aroused to come over despite this a sin but know I hate sharing wife even with myself this one I choice by myself okay first one once his so he said brother marry early I cook this one for you after divorce and find yours and I agree then he said okay if she wants but then I will give her but so Yahweh make her get pregnant early and he looked to the sky and clapped hands in anticipation now as I got up he said sit we talked for extra 10 minutes to clarify things and I said okay then he said my brother will not be interested in you because he has got his own wife but she like some else thats why he don't respect marriages so be mine only okay and our future is great and be with me forever other routes will lead to pain and sorrow and I said okay so let's go without great thought the only thing I had said that was to secure the job now that news of the job had come out more early why did I worry about sex I only said to do the opposite because I thought a jew would not do butt so I said let's go before the party started and I rose up and took my cream jacket and went to the bathroom to change soaked knickers and said I am ready to find a real man for I have the job to start a family and both looked at me and said okay how real you mean who don't like butt or not a and instantly I slapped him so hard that he staggered and said oh he'll jewel and

How To Find All Missing Persons / Unsolved Cases. And Collect All Reward Offers.
Volume XI. THE CASE OF ANNE CECILLE ZAPPELLI

cried for 2 seconds before he realised that we had a guest his brother and I said no talk of arse with me I need a baby and he kicked me in the leg and said break leg so we fuck all the time and they both started laughing I was about to laugh when he said okay let's go to the party and we went but there he had brought his wife and she was really pretty but with small shape lips and breasts so I understood why he needed another for I had a large chest and not sure about my vagina because I had not had sex so he said can we but at the party and I said look at her you do that to me when we are together then I will cut your dick off when you sleep and she he said oh my God I never do that to you and I said do that pointing yo my brother and I will cut your vagina out then she looked at me and covered her body and said howdie strettuvwxyz meaning my second sister wife and I said okay I love him so we will all be happy okay just don't give but to all but me and she said I never give anyone even myself and we all laughed then at 10.30 pm a man came and sat with me and said I can but how you can when all but then I said okay let's go but but 2 seconds but but he said okay but then he said if we then what but and I said if I then maybe but then he said what about these but but and I said tonight not even but but you can but only because vagina for him husband but and he said no way you 3 but why when we all are 0 buts then I froze and looked besides him and for the first time so another woman I mean a girl and said 2 come 3 want to ask questions and he said who 3 that's my daughter but and looked besides me and said oh you 3 me him and brother okay match but heart cut deep because now in public so maybe find him I am okay in public I refuse I have trust job if no one trust me then what house wife kids all want but now bye I never ask anything job you earned it no buts I love you bye and he cried hard and said okay I removed love Mark I give him no need to embrace me in public sorry and he knelt down and cried rubbing my buttocks that I became so aroused that I lifted him up and dragged him to corner and said don't cry but is here take all yours forever don't end us I love but this man once just to but just now and go and he said do you know him and I said no and he nearly slapped me and I said slap me you think you clean you want only loyal now if you want the but

How To Find All Missing Persons / Unsolved Cases. And Collect All Reward Offers.
Volume XI. THE CASE OF ANNE CECILLE ZAPPELLI

now or he will but but but but but buy because you talk but all the time and I am but and he said okay but never but so I call but good to but you but but but but but and he left and I cried for the first time then I heard a voice behind me saying bend down we but together because he is but and you are but but I but because you cry for but from brother and brother no but I know so bend double we but together and talk fir you only but now to us and I said I not but but you but and he said okay we go after this so you but but okay and lump moved down my heart and I said I love him but he don't like all who foes that who know you but God don't know you but then he waved and threw a kiss when I opened my eyes I was on the floor but nothing just laying there I tried to wake up but could not I tried lifting my head but could not now looking at it was it a dream or I had already died my vagina bleed blood not period blood and I lost everything I had a house at 27 Aterst
ANNE sterstuvwxyz rstuvwxyz who is buried at meterstuvwxyz Australia her electromagnetic wave number is 89286789832108928670186789088382108938678901 85
Phone number was 81768328416i76286789018326878926 4180 Australia first 12
Who killed her was artenopsr who said if I were you you would take car of that vagina and not give it to anyone now if we are to ask what can be then this is it we all can be
Yes I had a house at number 27 anterst and was left by my parents when they both died cancer did I had cancer I font know antersopsr because he said be careful or you will lose that vagina and I lost it what aty what happened cancer of the vagina so fast from the day a jew said watch that you might lose that vagina to the day she lay dead it was exactly 2 months 8 days they all said she was fit and well to take the job but the government had other plans her house to the government alone was worth 386987600 dollars because at the start when I knew her the house value was 8763210070083 dollars and this is because further won lottery then and bought the most expensive house in town and no one knew anything about the winning until when she came back from girls school then she was like a virgin and taking a job at the post office was a mistake what

ghey do is to give every rider who she save a cancer number everytime she serve them and over time this means post office font have to pay a lot of money and kill her early but Sergent astern ajern had other plans she was willing to marry a jew with his own wife and two kids that would have meant lose of the house and as such they are entitled to do her backside fast and a one way ticket to hell because God refuse butted women as you will never get these things in heaven now if we Asked what caused death then this is the answer she had the most aggressive for of cancer put in by arstenopqrst doctor akim a jew who specialized in cancers the code is 82386789018367890183218498687866789018423810098 now what you will witness has never been witnessed by any human being she had everything working well on day of first interview and asterposr warned that because she owned huge money in assets she might be targeted for the house so that people sell the house for capital gains tax and she said what do I do no man wants to marry me he said marry me when you find another then divorce sell the house and buy smaller and put money in the bank then the Sergent one day came and said jews don't pay taxes the fact that you are taking advice from the news means you are on a tax avoidance system as such you will not pay us but we can't let that happen we have never failed collecting taxes so you shall pay and now that day I received a code saying activate the cancer code above it was on Wednesday 2 August 1969 and she said what was that I felt like something just exploded in my vagina and fingers herself
instantly the slowest long.ago started but I could not understand a thing then so it actually said day of death is 21 September 1969 and I looked lost not that I have looks then instantly I started getting asked to start sending all messages abroad to [me- stoprstuvwxyz who I later knew as the queen of English land using port 7868901836789028658 and port 7898287648901832876189 now what surprised me is that I never come across a case when long.ago is used as a killing weapon because it never worked that way this time on day of death it said I am the jew version used by Yahweh to kill for sins like adultery and breaking up marriages if so then God

killed her but why now if we look at what the courts said it said that this long.ago start was indeed the cause of her death but Yahweh questioned everything about this case and said if it were adultery even so why the insistence of the two months yes sometimes Yahweh kill but why would he say die on 21 September 1969 it makes no sense if I am to check our records if his shallow prayer was answered then the answer is not a relied was sent from the reply angels who told me that nothing was ever acted on it brain scans revealed a joking part on the jew after all things that involve butts etc are not in the interest of Yahweh that means we must dig deeper to find out why this happened surely its a misconception that a prayer result in deaths that benefit those who prayed now if we look at the case as a whole then we must say that this case can be sent to other courts for clarification the reason being that in this case we can't be fairer in that if they say she died of the most aggressive cancers then talking about the jews prayer being the source then in this case then Yahweh can't be expected to judge fairly as such the case was sent to another chamber where we hope other intellectuals to look at the facts now this is what they found out they spent weeks looking at this case and gave us their verdict in which they said that it was Amy's missile that caused the cancer hence this had nothing to do with Yahweh Yahweh is still the merciful and righteous judge he will always be just and fair now that we can ask what happened with this woman Anne now after talking about but imitating the way gods speak then we can see a pattern imaging the branch post office manager want to help her keep the house by acting like her husband since as a jew he would be entitled now what can be will be as things turn out the two get involved romantically to share sex everyday in the house that in the end he brings the family to stay saying it's okay we are one big family now asking what can be then from now on he protected her from the police who wants money from the house sale but now not possible because realizing that she really love him and his wife and kids he plans to marry her in 8 months reduced to 6 after consultation with her and said can we but in 6 otherwise they might want to but in 4 or less like 2 which means targeting her for house sale even as less

How To Find All Missing Persons / Unsolved Cases. And Collect All Reward Offers. Volume XI. THE CASE OF ANNE CECILLE ZAPPELLI

as 2 months she said that so mean why is the house going anywhere why all of a sudden want to kill fast and he said to stop the marriage means house win and you dead and aty taking the body fast now if we Ask why this is so this the answer there is no time now it seems anteropsr's intervention was not to hell but to speed up things mind you just two months ago this woman was rock solid and all of a sudden she is so sick vagina drips blood to an extend that she can't hide it anymore not to anyone the public is shocked and ask what the hell is going on with you you were rock solid just a day ago it's like yesterday then she would say what a waste he like but and vagina cry blood of neglect now all the time what could be of vaginas with no one to love and for the first time aty said dead and buried and me riding your body as if I am you without the vagina because I want to be a boy and fuck rather than be fucked they fucked her for the house so I keep hearing and they are going to fuck her for the jew so I heard so how many fucks just one person all this for 283684898068 now let's look at this even more deeper we know now what they see doing going after orphans and stripping all property away leaving bare now if we Ask what happened this is the answer according to aty she was fucked twice for the house and for liking jews now these are Yahweh's favorite people from the time he was alone with Ibrahim the only man to live 10000 years because he understood what was needed and read the book of creation before his time of 100 days was over everytime he read it he got younger now let's look at what can be and what could be the woman is bleeding heavily according to the jew punishment by Yahweh for trying to break a relationship and to her her butt woes as now vagina is jealous to even stop bleeding as a way of attracting him because blood means have eggs all the time now if we Ask what can be them she can be divorced and remarried again that will stop the adultery charges now what can be of him without her no big loss but back to same old house and life that means even though the jew is blamed for everything he literally has nothing to gain so who gains from her death if we look closer she is rich I meant he wealthiest in 10 counties biggest the father won lottery and saved everything scare to get a long.ago started on himself he secretly

How To Find All Missing Persons / Unsolved Cases. And Collect All Reward Offers.
Volume XI. THE CASE OF ANNE CECILLE ZAPPELLI

bought a house and put his daughters name when she was 9 and then said reveal only at 19 birthday and all of a sudden she don't need a job the manager gave her a job at 17 years 1 year early due to religion and not start laws that say at 18 years old should a woman start work in Australia all this facilitated by aty which turned out that he was created what he said restore points that can't be removed in that every time he put a restore point that means before that he can't go back there now what is interesting is that he is asking everyone what to do and how to fix her fast because as it turns out these people programmed the robot to want a sex change in the end that means when it wants the body it will want the destruction of sex organs which then becomes his passion as its a boy in a girl's dress meaning she wanted to be a man but woke up a girl to correct is to get all sex organs removed I'm normal circumstances this would not be possible because the boy will want to continue as a boy if in a boys body and vice versa now let's look what happens after when they fell in love he didn't want to get her pregnant and his reason was that he could not afford it as the post office was a family run business as the dole trader his wages were not up to to-date his excuse he got her at a younger age where can employ but pay 2 dollars less until 22 but at 19 she discovered that she is a billionaire to everyone's shock now the day she discovered she was a billionaire everyone else knew that means those who wanted their capital gains tax wanted their cut there before the house is lot to others hence there has no an attempt to kill in the history of mankind than this time billions drove these mad literally mad as you will see at the end a couple of doctors gathered at the university of Queensland and spoke and all agreed and all said in the name of saving life's we can test a new super virus to change habits a rich woman who use money to destroy a family is worse than the devil therefore she must end in long slow long.ago and these are people are
1 dr sternspt
2 dr derstopnt
3 dr dedomnop
4 dr ertestuvw

How To Find All Missing Persons / Unsolved Cases. And Collect All Reward Offers. Volume XI. THE CASE OF ANNE CECILLE ZAPPELLI

5 dr cteropqrstuvwxyz [riverband]
6 dr sturstuvwxyz
7 dr ntopqrstuvw
8 dr mnoprtuvwst ,[cleanwater]
9 strong
10 vuwxyrtstuvwxyz [sugarnote]

Now why raising this issue is the fact that in this long.ago she will never recover but die so as it tens out all the language of the gods was actually commands to self terminate and on the other side incapacitate as it turns out in that a normal women never-ending rich could not speak a proper language but keep saying buts but this was a sign of unrecognized illness that will make it hard in the future for her to speak associated with rich people who now can't think of anything to drive them now the brain starts to deteriorate all this for a promised huge donation by a one artest-pern who happened to be the beneficiary because he fuck her for sex and she said if I die can you bury me in the church that will be awesome because everything is stopping the farming has not stopped my vagina froze I had to keep slapping it before aty start again by the way who has aty that kill you and gloat about how fast it was in getting rid of you according to them now after discovering that I am a billionaire I was expected to live around 70 years more but that day I heard a strange noise and a long.ago start that said soon after that day of death 21 September 1969 at 13.04 hrs in maceteataburel Australia I am going to be a boy again a human that can think and talk and say I love you to a real vagina and put it on toast and say bye vagina men go without se x for such a long time but I fix vagina and say I want dick for me and butt for my dick end of vagina then instance now let's look deeper for the last time

The fact is that when she died it was exactly 64 days since the day she was told that she had received a house worth thousand dollars that means even though they had said billions it was now

Now when the man came we had sex and he said ooh why so horny but it's strangely warm like are you having your periods and I said no and then I said what about us I never said this to anyone and what is long start aty their thing they put inside me that talk keeps

How To Find All Missing Persons / Unsolved Cases. And Collect All Reward Offers.
Volume XI. THE CASE OF ANNE CECILLE ZAPPELLI

asking for status long.ago and I can actually here like my body saying days but now counting down but fast and he said what long.ago start instantly I spoke but it was not me and said 2 days 6 hours 23 minutes and 10 seconds counting this will set a new record at the university of Queensland that I will be given the acetate award as the fastest killing acetate ever her with her billions sat on them until death if she was clever than me she could have sold the house and hire expects to fight me until death and it said what can we do and it said humans will always die but we acetate will always be there but in the history on mankind there is no better record where I reduce a billionaire to a shell and hip of blood and pussy and blinked not winked that it was just a joke the bleeding did not stop and whatever it said would only increase the blood flow but out for sure I was okay then not even thinking of death but everyday I bleed fast it would smile like a boy and said vagina I can see you go bye bitch I never want to see you smelly and he said I just received a message from doctor artopen saying if I can dance as well that will be great because we need a great record and he said she said how is she doing is she doing great and said great maybe billions work for real I have never danced so much yet she is smiling like as if but I dance and instant I screamed because of the amount of blood oozing out I realised it was the dancing I thought it was to cheer me up but what can you do if it's something inside you so I cried until another beep and I asked who and he said dr stern saying I might lose this competition now he danced morning and day but it never felt like until I ran out of blood i knew it and asked for blood donors and 10 were waiting for me to ask and I got better but now he dance and I strangle the place until a little boy say how can I when you keep stopping me and the last time I punched hard that I broke something inside me he laughed and said see I am smarter than him she broke her own pelvis for being stupid see money does not mean brains this shit is proof now if you let me let me take the body I will be much happy please I slowed down for the body if I had accelerated for the price you could be in church by now so I said why church and he said because the church is where you said you want to be buried I slapped it hard and it frowned so hard and I died

I woke up here now can we appoint blame to the doctors especially doctor artenop and stern who contributed by coaching and encouraging it the answer I think the last time yes because she died quickly and soon after now what can we say about this case it is the typical thieving of orphans this time a huge jackpot indeed going into trillions 9876854381680 such a some has never been heard of ever again even up to now this is still the biggest bank robbery by far now let's look at other people we can add to this list the jew is guilty of fast forward things for a 8% cut after 8 years which he accepted to the court's dismay in 1077 in May of 280198 now what can we say about him in court he was served with a 2 year jail term even then but for different reasons then he was accused of plighing her with wine when she was in pain instead of taking her to a doctor waiting for her to die now what can say about doctor rosteop he was to be sentenced to 11 years in jail when he died admitted administering a highly lethal code with aim to kill fast and break record this lacks professionalism

THE KILLER AND THE COORDINATES

Now who is the real one killer this court has chosen astern ajern who is a computer program designed to kill and hide evidence working through its protégé atn to kill his reward a body of a female when he is a man meaning he will also have to find ways to remove sex organs waiting for his big dick that penetrates and rotates even deeper to give the best satisfaction but we hold the police to account especially Pc artenop who said if she marry that jew we lost the first trillionaire jew we all go bankrupt so act fast make that phone call to dr asteop now lastly who got the house it was the same police man Pc asteop but lived there for 5 years before he sold it left the office and lived happily ever after if we asked at what price he got it at 24867890 but on loan it said meaning without paying anything then sold it for 78658980182 to the bank for cash making him the only millionaire who ever existed but never hears of the money after but soon after a huge residential area got erected at 08092867498773867128489772807286380982 80
Now his electromagnetic number is 86778928471836285178184982836841992863289841207869 if we Ask her to look at him
I died I was killed for the house officer astern ajern leaked information to Pc asteop who was also a doctor now what can be of police officer who kill for a piece of land and an orphan to make things worse in broad light breaking death record these must rot in hell until the end of time so far we had most of these shelved in hell to burn forever now we want the closing stages to be real to take to

How To Find All Missing Persons / Unsolved Cases. And Collect All Reward Offers. Volume XI. THE CASE OF ANNE CECILLE ZAPPELLI

court and kill within less than 6 months quartered to 1.25 months I understand that there were systems in the past that let those with to walk away even involved as the I
Asked what caused death then this is the answer she had the most aggressive for of cancer put in by arstenopqrst doctor akim a jew who specialized in cancers the code is 8238678901836789018321849868786678901842381098 now what you will witness has never been witnessed by any human being she had everything working well on day of first interview and asterposr warned that because she owned huge money in assets she might be targeted for the house so that people sell the house for capital gains tax and she said what do I do no man wants to marry me he said marry me when you find another then divorce sell the house and buy smaller and put money in the bank then the Sergent one day came and said jews don't pay taxes the fact that you are taking advice from the news means you are on a tax avoidance system as such you will not pay us but we can't let that happen we have never failed collecting taxes so you shall pay and now that day I received a code saying activate the cancer code above it was on Wednesday 2 August 1969 and she said what was that I felt like something just exploded in my vagina and fingers herself
instantly the slowest long.ago started but I could not understand a thing then so it actually said day of death is 21 September 1969 and I looked lost not that I have looks then instantly I started getting asked to start sending all messages abroad to [me- stoprstuvwxyz who I later knew as the queen of English land using port 7868901836789028658 and port [7898287648901832876189 now what surprised me is that I never come across a case when long.ago is used as a killing weapon because it never worked that way this time on day of death it said I am the jew version used by Yahweh to kill for sins like adultery and breaking up marriages if so then God killed her but why now if we look at what the courts said it said that this long start was indeed the cause of her death but Yahweh questioned everything about this case and said if it were adultery even so why the insistence of the two months yes sometimes Yahweh kill but why would he say die on 21 September 1969 it

makes no sense if I am to check our records if his shallow prayer was answered then the answer is not a relied was sent from the reply angels who told me that nothing was ever acted on it brain scans revealed a joking part on the jew after all things that involve butts etc are not in the interest of Yahweh that means we must dig deeper to find out why this happened]

THE CLAIM

the reward offer

THE COLLECTION

www.twofuture.world/donate

ABOUT DAVID GOMADZA

visit www.twofuture.world

signed david gomadza
ask.davidgomadzaauthorised.licensed.checkya.askya.ya

- 23may23.42pm

scotland
00447719210295
davidgomadza@hotmail.com
info@twofuture.world

www.ingramcontent.com/pod-product-compliance
Lightning Source LLC
Chambersburg PA
CBHW031517210526
45464CB00007B/2944